PIANO · VOCAL · GUITAR

A SENTIMENTAL CHRISTMAS

ISBN 978-1-4950-9703-4

HAL•LEONARD®

7777 W. BLUEMOUND RD. P.O. BOX 13819 MILWAUKEE, WI 53213

Visit Hal Leonard Online at
www.halleonard.com

CONTENTS

ALL I WANT FOR CHRISTMAS IS YOU

Words and Music by MARIAH CAREY
and WALTER AFANASIEFF

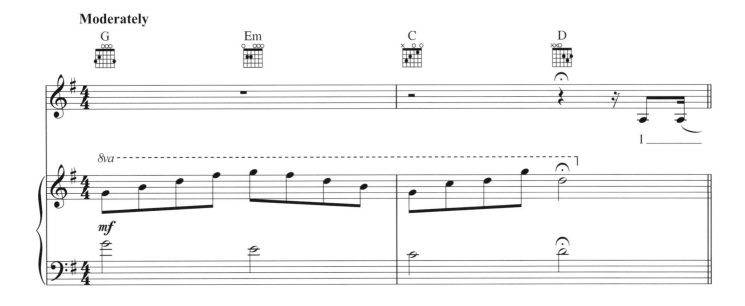

don't want a lot for _____ Christ-mas, there _____ is just one thing I _____ need. _____

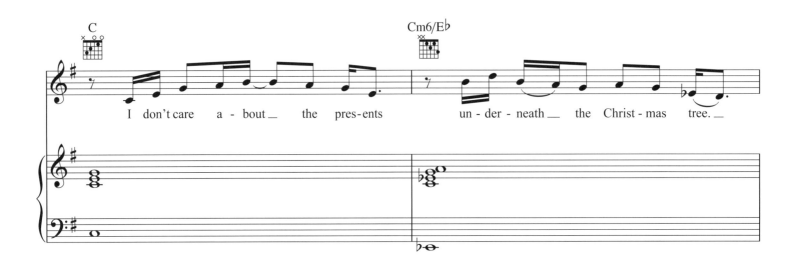

I don't care a-bout _____ the pres-ents un-der-neath _____ the Christ-mas tree. _____

THE CHRISTMAS SONG
(Chestnuts Roasting on an Open Fire)

Music and Lyric by MEL TORMÉ
and ROBERT WELLS

BLUE CHRISTMAS

Words and Music by BILLY HAYES
and JAY JOHNSON

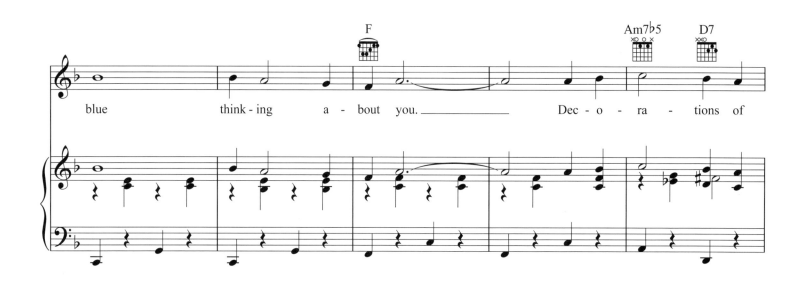

CHRISTMAS LIGHTS

Words and Music by GUY BERRYMAN,
WILL CHAMPION, CHRIS MARTIN
and JONNY BUCKLAND

Still wait-ing for the snow to fall, __ it does-n't real-ly feel __ like Christ - mas at all. __

Those Christ - mas lights light up the street,
lights light up the street,
lights, light up the street,

A little slower, with a lilt

THE CHRISTMAS SHOES

Words and Music by LEONARD AHLSTROM
and EDDIE CARSWELL

CHRISTMASES WHEN YOU WERE MINE

Words and Music by NATHAN CHAPMAN,
LIZ ROSE and TAYLOR SWIFT

Moderately

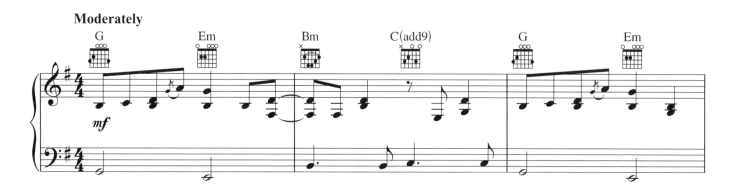

Please take down the mis - tle - toe, _____ 'cause

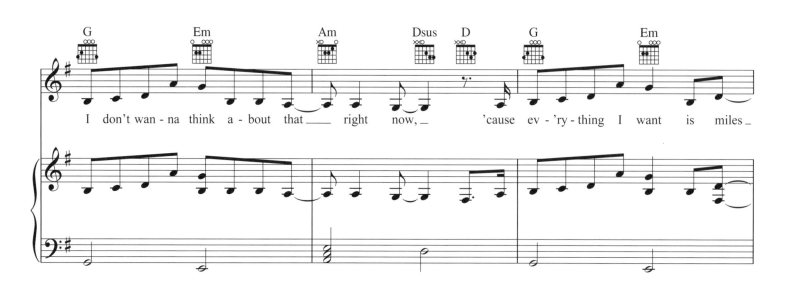

I don't wan - na think a - bout that ___ right now, ___ 'cause ev - 'ry - thing I want is miles ___

FAIRYTALE OF NEW YORK

Words and Music by JEREMY FINER
and SHANE MacGOWAN

sing-ing___ "Gal - way Bay." And the bells___ were ring-ing out____ for Christ-mas Day.___

Female: 5. You're a

Additional Lyrics

2. Got on a lucky one, came in eighteen to one;
I've got a feeling this year's for me and you.
So happy Christmas; I love you, baby.
I can see a better time when all our dreams come true.

5. *(Female)* You're a bum, you're a punk!
(Male) You're an old slut on junk
Lying there almost dead on a drip in that bed!
(Female) You scumbag! You maggot!
You cheap lousy faggot!
Happy Christmas your arse!
I pray God it's our last.

GROWN-UP CHRISTMAS LIST

Words and Music by DAVID FOSTER
and LINDA THOMPSON-JENNER

on-ly in __ our blind be-lief __ can we ev-er find __ the truth.

No more lives __ torn a-part, __ and wars would nev - er

start, and time would heal __ all hearts. And ev - 'ry-one would have __ a friend, __

CHRISTMAS TIME IS HERE

from A CHARLIE BROWN CHRISTMAS

Words by LEE MENDELSON
Music by VINCE GUARALDI

HAPPY XMAS
(War Is Over)

Written by JOHN LENNON
and YOKO ONO

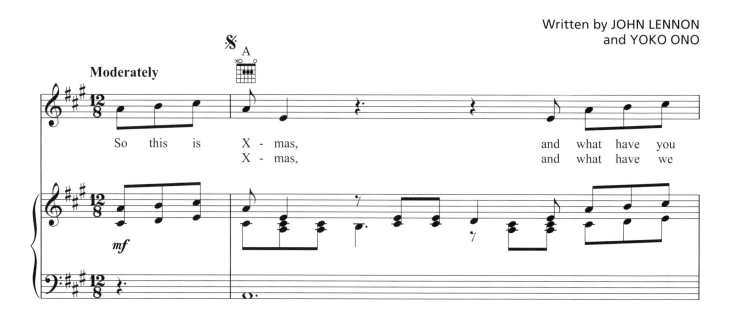

So this is X - mas, and what have you
X - mas, and what have we

done? An - oth - er year o - ver, a new one just be-
done? An - oth - er year o - ver, a new one just be-

gun. _____ And so this is X - mas; I hope you have
gun. _____ And so hap - py X - mas; we hope you have

HAVE YOURSELF A MERRY LITTLE CHRISTMAS

from MEET ME IN ST. LOUIS

Words and Music by HUGH MARTIN
and RALPH BLANE

Lyrics: When the stee-ple bells sound their "A," they don't play it in tune.

(There's No Place Like)
HOME FOR THE HOLIDAYS

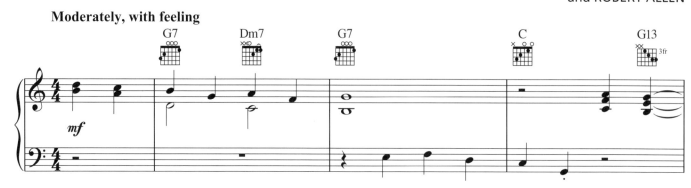

Words and Music by AL STILLMAN
and ROBERT ALLEN

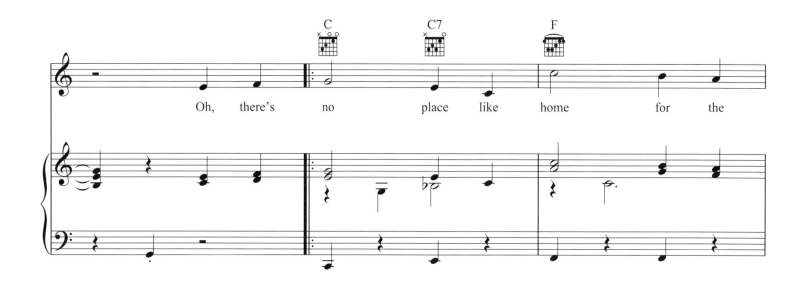

Oh, there's no place like home for the

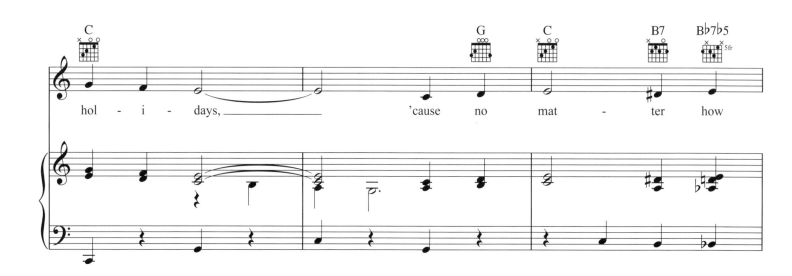

hol-i-days, _____ 'cause no mat-ter how

I'LL BE HOME FOR CHRISTMAS

Words and Music by KIM GANNON
and WALTER KENT

I HEARD THE BELLS ON CHRISTMAS DAY

Words by HENRY WADSWORTH LONGFELLOW
Adapted by JOHNNY MARKS
Music by JOHNNY MARKS

I WISH IT COULD BE CHRISTMAS ALL YEAR LONG

Words and Music by
PHIL BARON

IT MUST HAVE BEEN THE MISTLETOE
(Our First Christmas)

Words and Music by JUSTIN WILDE
and DOUG KONECKY

ONE LITTLE CHRISTMAS TREE

Words and Music by RONALD N. MILLER
and BRYAN WELLS

One lit-tle Christ-mas tree was stand-ing a - lone, __
One lit-tle an - gel who was rid-ing a star __

wait - ing for some - one to come by.
cried as she looked down at the tree. Oh,

One lit - tle Christ - mas tree that nev - er had grown
please, Mis - ter Fa - ther Tree, wher - ev - er you are,

PLEASE COME HOME FOR CHRISTMAS

Words and Music by CHARLES BROWN
and GENE REDD

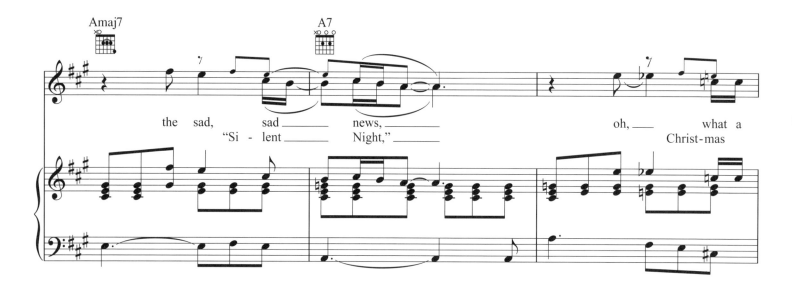

MERRY CHRISTMAS, DARLING

Words and Music by RICHARD CARPENTER
and FRANK POOLER

SAME OLD LANG SYNE

Words and Music by
DAN FOGELBERG

Met my old lov - er in the gro - c'ry store. ___
She did - n't rec - og - nize the face at first, ___
Instrumental
We took her gro - c'ries to the check - out stand; ___
We went to have our - selves a drink or two, ___
She said she's mar - ried her an ar - chi - tect, ___
I said the years had been a friend to her ___
She said she saw me in the rec - ord stores, ___

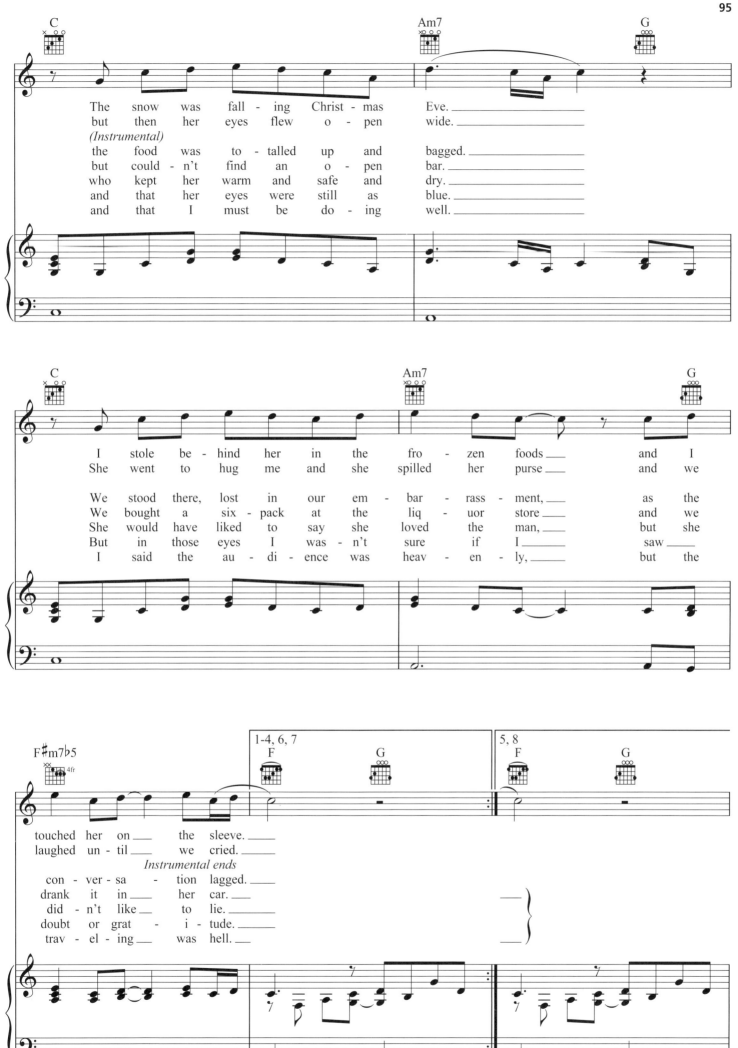

SILVER BELLS
from the Paramount Picture THE LEMON DROP KID

Words and Music by JAY LIVINGSTON
and RAY EVANS

SOMEWHERE IN MY MEMORY

from the Twentieth Century Fox Motion Picture HOME ALONE

Words by LESLIE BRICUSSE
Music by JOHN WILLIAMS

THERE'S STILL MY JOY

Words and Music by MELISSA MANCHESTER,
MATT ROLLINGS and BETH CHAPMAN

Simply, with feeling

I brought my tree down to the shore, the gar-land and the sil-ver

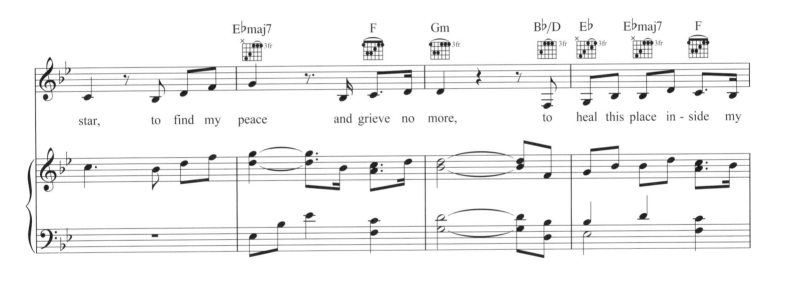

star, to find my peace and grieve no more, to heal this place in-side my

heart. On ev-'ry branch, I laid some bread, and hun-gry birds filled up the

TENNESSEE CHRISTMAS

Words and Music by AMY GRANT
and GARY CHAPMAN

Moderate 4

Come on weath-er-man ___ give us ___ a fore-
Ev-'ry now ___ and then ___ I get ___ a wan-

-cast snow-y white. ___
-derin' urge ___ to see,

Can't you hear ___ the prayers ___ of ev-'ry child-
may-be Cal-i-for-nia, may-be Tin-

YOU'RE ALL I WANT FOR CHRISTMAS

Words and Music by GLEN MOORE
and SEGER ELLIS

Ad lib., dreamily

WHERE ARE YOU CHRISTMAS?

from DR. SEUSS' HOW THE GRINCH STOLE CHRISTMAS

Words and Music by WILL JENNINGS,
JAMES HORNER and MARIAH CAREY

WHITE CHRISTMAS

from the Motion Picture Irving Berlin's HOLIDAY INN

Words and Music by
IRVING BERLIN

The sun is shin - ing, the grass is green, — the or - ange and palm trees sway. There's nev - er been such a day in Bev - er - ly Hills, L. A.

Christmas Collections

from Hal Leonard

All books arranged for piano, voice & guitar.

All-Time Christmas Favorites – Second Edition

This second edition features an all-star lineup of 32 Christmas classics, including: Blue Christmas • The Chipmunk Song • The Christmas Song • Frosty the Snow Man • Here Comes Santa Claus • I Saw Mommy Kissing Santa Claus • Jingle-Bell Rock • Let It Snow! Let It Snow! Let It Snow! • Merry Christmas, Darling • Nuttin' for Christmas • Rockin' Around the Christmas Tree • Rudolph the Red-Nosed Reindeer • Santa, Bring My Baby Back (To Me) • There Is No Christmas like a Home Christmas • and more.
00359051..$14.99

The Best Christmas Songs Ever – 6th Edition

69 all-time favorites are included in the 6th edition of this collection of Christmas tunes. Includes: Auld Lang Syne • Coventry Carol • Frosty the Snow Man • Happy Holiday • It Came Upon the Midnight Clear • O Holy Night • Rudolph the Red-Nosed Reindeer • Silver Bells • What Child Is This? • and many more.
00359130..$24.99

The Big Book of Christmas Songs – 2nd Edition

An outstanding collection of over 120 all-time Christmas favorites and hard-to-find classics. Features: Angels We Have Heard on High • As Each Happy Christmas • Auld Lang Syne • The Boar's Head Carol • Christ Was Born on Christmas Day • Bring a Torch Jeannette, Isabella • Carol of the Bells • Coventry Carol • Deck the Halls • The First Noel • The Friendly Beasts • God Rest Ye Merry Gentlemen • I Heard the Bells on Christmas Day • It Came Upon a Midnight Clear • Jesu, Joy of Man's Desiring • Joy to the World • Masters in This Hall • O Holy Night • The Story of the Shepherd • 'Twas the Night Before Christmas • What Child Is This? • and many more. Includes guitar chord frames.
00311520..$19.95

Christmas Songs – Budget Books

Save some money this Christmas with this fabulous budget-priced collection of 100 holiday favorites: All I Want for Christmas Is You • Christmas Time Is Here • Feliz Navidad • Grandma Got Run Over by a Reindeer • Happy Holiday • I'll Be Home for Christmas • Jesus Born on This Day • Last Christmas • Merry Christmas, Baby • O Holy Night • Please Come Home for Christmas • Rockin' Around the Christmas Tree • Some Children See Him • We Need a Little Christmas • What Child Is This? • and more.
00310887..$12.99

The Definitive Christmas Collection – 3rd Edition

Revised with even more Christmas classics, this must-have 3rd edition contains 127 top songs, such as: Blue Christmas • Christmas Time Is Here • Do You Hear What I Hear • The First Noel • A Holly Jolly Christmas • Jingle-Bell Rock • Little Saint Nick • Merry Christmas, Darling • O Holy Night • Rudolph, the Red-Nosed Reindeer • Silver and Gold • We Need a Little Christmas • You're All I Want for Christmas • and more!
00311602..$24.95

The Most Requested Christmas Songs

This giant collection features nearly 70 holiday classics, from traditional carols to modern Christmas hits: Blue Christmas • Christmas Time Is Here • Deck the Hall • Feliz Navidad • I'll Be Home for Christmas • Jingle Bells • Little Saint Nick • Nuttin' for Christmas • Rudolph the Red-Nosed Reindeer • Silent Night • and more.
00001563..$19.99

The Muppet Christmas Carol

Matching folio to the blockbuster movie featuring 11 Muppet carols and eight pages of color photos. Bless Us All • Chairman of the Board • Christmas Scat • Finale - When Love Is Found/It Feels like Christmas • It Feels like Christmas • Marley and Marley • One More Sleep 'Til Christmas • Room in Your Heart • Scrooge • Thankful Heart • When Love Is Gone.
00312483..$16.99

Tim Burton's The Nightmare Before Christmas

This book features 11 songs from Tim Burton's creepy animated classic, with music and lyrics by Danny Elfman. Songs include: Jack's Lament • Jack's Obsession • Kidnap the Sandy Claws • Making Christmas • Oogie Boogie's Song • Poor Jack • Sally's Song • This Is Halloween • Town Meeting Song • What's This? • Finale/Reprise.
00312488..$14.99

Ultimate Christmas – 3rd Edition

100 seasonal favorites: Auld Lang Syne • Bring a Torch, Jeannette, Isabella • Carol of the Bells • The Chipmunk Song • Christmas Time Is Here • The First Noel • Frosty the Snow Man • Gesù Bambino • Happy Holiday • Happy Xmas (War Is Over) • Hymne • Jesu, Joy of Man's Desiring • Jingle-Bell Rock • March of the Toys • My Favorite Things • The Night Before Christmas Song • Pretty Paper • Silver and Gold • Silver Bells • Suzy Snowflake • What Child Is This • The Wonderful World of Christmas • and more.
00361399 ....$21.99

HAL•LEONARD®